Buzz the Bot

by Karra McFarlane

illustrated by Jennifer Naalchigar

OXFORD
UNIVERSITY PRESS
AUSTRALIA & NEW ZEALAND

Zak gets a big box.

Jen gets a box.

She sits a box on top.

Zak gets lots of cups.

Zak gets an egg box.
He taps it onto the leg.

Jen dabs dots.

She dabs a zigzag.

Jen and Zak will not quit.

He can fizz.

Buzz is quick!

Buzz wins!